By His Grace

A Memoir about Surviving Childhood Domestic Violence and Sexual Assault

Jacqueline Williams

Copyright @ 2023 Jacqueline Williams, All rights reserved.
ISBN: 979-8878902717

This book is dedicated in the loving memory to my sister, Lucille.
We planned to co-author this book, but in February 1998, Lucille passed away.

"We are confident, I say, and willing rather to be absent from the body, and to be present with the Lord" (2 Corinthians 5:6-8 KJV)

"We put our hope in the Lord. He is our hope and our shield. In Him our hearts rejoice, for we trust in His holy name. Let your unfailing love surround us, Lord. For our hope is in you alone" (Psalms 33:20-22 NLT).

Contents

Chapter 1 1
   The Dark Years 1

Chapter 2 22
   The Middle Passage 22

Chapter 3 29
   Spiraling 29

Chapter 4 31
   Deliverance 31

Chapter 5 36
   The After Glow 36

About The Author 42

Chapter 1

The Dark Years

I remember saying to my sister, "We should begin the book with *'the real Amityville Horror lived at our house but nobody knew.'*"

She answered, *"Ain't that the truth."*

However, this memoir is not about the horror of our childhood. It's not about the pain and depravity we endured. It's about triumph and the depth of God's incredible, amazing, unfailing love for us. It's about our victorious journey to Jesus.

And Hezekiah prayed to the Lord: "Lord, the God of Israel, enthroned between the cherubim, you alone are God over all the kingdoms of the earth. You have made heaven and earth" (2 Kings 19:15 NIV).

"As for you, you were dead in your transgressions and sins, in which you used to live when you followed the ways of this world and of the ruler of the kingdom of the air, the spirit who is now at work in those who are disobedient. All of us also lived among them at one time, gratifying the cravings of our sinful nature and following its desires and thoughts. Like the rest, we were by nature objects of wrath. But because of His great love for us, God, who is

rich in mercy, made us alive with Christ even when we were dead in our transgressions–it is by grace you have been saved" (Ephesians 2:1-5 NIV).

On a lovely street in the suburbs of Long Island, New York, inside a nicely decorated three-bedroom house with a manicured lawn and a swing set in the backyard, you would never think evil thrived there. Have you ever heard people speak of being on the devil's *hit list*? Well, that was the case with us. The devil definitely had a *hit* on me, my mom, and my sister. However, because we belonged to God, the *hit* mangled us. It cut us deeply. Ultimately, it failed. Let's start with Mama. Life in Brooklyn must have seemed really fast, fun, and exciting to a pretty teenager from Boydton, Virginia back in the 1940's. By 1945, when she was only 18 years old, our mama began dating a married man and soon discovered she was pregnant with my sister. Ten years later, she met and married my father, but their marriage didn't last very long. For years, Mama told me very little about my father. She said she left him because he was a *Mama's boy*, and she didn't like his mother. She didn't tell me that she behaved as if she wasn't married and did as she pleased. From first-hand experience, I can say she had great difficulty loving anyone the right way. She actually had no clue. She loved me and my sister, and she sometimes tried her best to show it. Unfortunately, she often demonstrated her love in the worst way. She was so jealous of Lucille's natural beauty that she rarely tried to show her any love at all. I don't think our mother had any real sense of how to be a mother.

There are many women who give birth to children but really shouldn't. Sadly, that was the case with our mother. Don't get me wrong, we loved her. As I said, she loved us too, but it wasn't enough to put us first. So, was what she shared *real love* or something else Mama was taught at a young age. As adults, we often mimic what we see as children, whether the actions are ignorant, incomplete, adequate, or wonderful.

Mama didn't know any better, so she did what she knew. We were caught in what she knew and we were trapped. Approximately four million referrals for alleged maltreatment are made to child protective services agencies each year. Mama was a good mother in many other ways. We had nice clothes. She cooked the very best meals, and she was affectionate and in many ways one of the kindest people (almost to a fault) you'd ever meet. Mama was hardworking and very book smart. I think she was some kind of mathematical genius because she devised a system that outwit illegal numbers back in the day and won regularly. Mama would have enjoyed developing a system to win within our modern-day lottery.

She was definitely a free spirit, broken by a mad-man, or perhaps she was broken way before she met him. That breaking may have happened in the red hills of southern Virginia. As kids, we traveled to Boydton often, and we had many happy times with family and friends there. I actually live about 15-20 miles north of Boydton now. It's a quiet rural community, and it's very different from anywhere I've ever lived. It's nice living close to my family, but there is definitely that *overt racist vibe* here. You can literally feel the hate.

When our grandmother was alive, life felt safer. For years, she was our anchor. There was Grandma, Aunt Kitty, and Aunt Mae. I thank God for my honest aunts. I was nearly thirty years old when my Aunt Mae told me the truth about my parents. She said, "The two main reasons your parent's marriage didn't work were because your mama cheated on your father more than once. No matter what she did or said, your father would not beat her. He didn't believe a man should ever hit a woman. Nothing she did could make him hit her, not even when one of her old boyfriends came to visit, and she asked her husband to get up out of their bed so the former boyfriend (who used to beat her up) could lie down and rest. Aunt Mae explained that my father had worked all night at Con Edison and was clearly tired, but he got up and gave his spot in their bed to *Slim*.

Aunt Mae thought my father left almost too quietly that morning. She said he held me, he kissed me, hugged Lucille, gave her some money, and made her promise to take care of us. I was about two years old, and Lucille was ten, almost eleven. Aunt Mae also said he came back every Friday to give her money for me and Lucille. But he never came back to stay, and he timed his visits so he never saw Mama. My Aunt Kitty told me that *Slim* (the old boyfriend who came to *visit*) had previously kidnapped my mother, tied her to a chair, and held her hostage with a gun to her head in an abandoned warehouse for days because he was so insanely jealous and thought she was flirting with other men. So, my father left and never spoke to me, Lucille, or our mother again. My father seemed so deeply hurt that it was easier for him to forget my deeply troubled mother and everything attached to her. But easier for who? I think giving my aunt money for us was good, especially because Lucille was clearly not his child. That sort of noble gesture still didn't absolve him from wrong-doing. While he lived safely in Brooklyn with his new wife and sons, less than an hour away, we lived in true horror every single day and every single night.

From age three until 22, my father never said a word to me. I saw him once when I was six years old at his sister's funeral. At the tender age of six, I recognized him from their wedding picture. He never knew how I desperately wanted and needed him to scoop me up in his arms at that funeral. He never even looked at me. I kept that picture in my bedroom. I looked at and touched it with my little hand for many years. On his death bed, with just days to live, he asked a friend of the family to find me and ask me to come to the hospital. I was out of town. He died. I was 22 years old, and I finally put the picture away, knowing there would be no rescue, no reconciliation, and no father's love for a left behind *Daddy's girl*. He also never knew I was beaten and sexually assaulted repeatedly. I was abused (almost beyond repair) over and over by two men I should have been able to trust. No, he never know but my heavenly Father knew all about it.

When I was about 3 years old, we moved from Brooklyn, New York to Amityville, Long Island. We lived on Bayview Avenue, and during that time, it was just the three of us: Mama, Lucille, and me. My mom and my sister had a lot of problems. Our mother was a pretty woman, and my sister inherited her looks and then some. Sadly, most of her life, Mama treated Lucille terribly. She always behaved as if she loved me more. I guess my average looks paid off in that regard. Mama and Lucille even had physical fights. Sadly, my sister had very little to no respect for our mother. It was mostly because she had not been a real mother to Lucille and behaved more like a wayward friend-enemy, but I have to admit, I really don't remember being afraid when it was just the three of us.

The days filled with fear came later when I was about 4 years old. My mother met a *madman* named Howard Parks. I clearly remember him molesting me around age ten, but my therapist explained it began when I was much younger, probably around age 5 because of a scene in a recurring nightmare I had well into my twenties. In that nightmare, I was very small and very afraid. My height reached near Howard's knees. The molestation happened so many times, more times than I can count, mostly because Mama always left me alone with him. She even sent me with him at night on overnight trips. It also happened whenever she wasn't at home, which was often. I believe she was happy not to have to take care of her own child and wanted to be free to do whatever she wanted. Many parents just want and need a little break from their kids every now and then. However, you must be very careful who you allow to care for your children, even for short periods of time. Another reason Mama sent me with him was so she could find out if Howard had been intimate with other women. Too bad other women weren't all he wanted. Too bad she didn't care more about me and my sister than Howard and other women.

When I was about ten years old our mother caught Howard fondling me in their bed with his penis between my legs. When Mama caught him fondling me, her first words to me were, "Mommy doesn't like the t*hings you do*."

Those words sounded like she blamed me just like she blamed my sister when Lucille jumped from Howard's moving car to escape rape. Lucille looked like a grown woman. She was in high school by then, and she knew she would get more than fondling, so she opened the car door and jumped. I remember how she threw-up afterwards. She shared that he drove faster and the sick way he laughed when she opened the car door. She ran to my grandmother's house, stockings ripped, knees bloody and face scraped. Mama saw her, heard her but didn't believe her. So, Lucille fell in love, got pregnant, and was married at 17. She didn't graduate from high school and forgot about her dream of becoming a registered nurse. I always felt she got out the only way she knew how. Unfortunately, I was still trapped. My sister's first husband, Ben, was an ambitious would-be golf pro. My cousin Danny once said Ben was the first Tiger Woods, and Danny was one of the smartest men I have ever known. He was sure if Ben had come up in a different era he would have become sports rich and famous.

For a long time, no matter how she tried to be okay, Lucille was very unhappy because of the kind of life we had with our mother always putting her current man's needs ahead her children. The damage was done. Lucille was 9 years older than me and had gone through so much more until Howard that is. Consequently, we both had little to no self-esteem, and we learned very early on to mask our thoughts and our feelings.

Lucille's drug of choice was alcohol and mine was cocaine. She attempted suicide twice. Thank God, that was not the Lord's plan for her life. Alcohol became her constant companion and cocaine became mine. Lucille also had a heart of gold and was one of the most patient people you'd ever want to meet, but the damage done to her was more than love and marriage could repair. Her first husband wasn't a bad guy. Ben liked everyone and always treated people with such kindness, and they had three great kids. He was more like a brother than a brother-in-law.

In the beginning, he spent all his free time with his wife and kids, trying to make a good life for them. In the end, he failed at saving Lucille and reverted back to the charming, life of the party cheater she met at the bowling alley. They had many happy times, but after 15 years and a lot of problems, they divorced. Years later, Lucille met and married a man who adored her. She also accepted the Lord Jesus Christ as her personal savior just before she met her second husband, and they had a good marriage until she passed away in 1998. Lucille lived one year after she was diagnosed with ovarian cancer. It was my privilege to be there with her from the beginning to the end. Ovarian cancer is an aggressive devastating cancer, but we were able to share some fun and lots of laughs before the hospice stage. My sister and I nicknamed Howard, 'The Real Amityville Horror" after the movie we had many conversations about. We discussed how the author of the book and producers of the movie totally missed the real horror story that took place in Amityville.

For me, the molestation continued for years until one extremely cold winter day. Everything in Amityville was under a blanket of knee-high white snow. That day, as usual, Mama left me home alone with him. I was sitting on my bed quietly reading a book. He walked into my room and attacked me. I didn't know what I'd done wrong. He never said a word, but I was old enough now to know this was real danger. As usual, Howard began trying to molest me, but this time I fought him. Every instinct in me knew this was wrong, and I wouldn't be still. Because I would not cooperate, he hit me and knocked me down. I hit the floor hard. My head hurt, and I was dazed and confused. I was so scared and did not understand why this was happening to me. I remember how he glared at me, probably because I had never fought before. I always froze and sat still, absolutely, terrified, and completely immobile, allowing him to do what he pleased but not this time.

Next, he snatched me up from the floor by the neck so violently that the inside of my jaw ripped. I can still remember the pain in the back of my head as I hit the floor. I was having difficulty breathing, and there was a taste of blood in my mouth. I was so terrified I became nauseous, but I couldn't even scream. He kept hitting me, and it hurt more than words can say. He was 6 feet tall and about 175-225 lbs. I was skinny little, 12-year-old kid. I was less than 5 feet tall and probably weighed 85, maybe 90 lbs. He choked me. As he carried me into the bedroom by the neck with my feet dangling in the air, I felt I was dying. I heard my own sobs and gasps for air. I wondered, *Why is this happening?*

As he was taking off my pants, the doorbell rang. It was a very cold New York winter, and there was about two or three feet of snow outside. No one was really out visiting neighbors. Thank God! The person at the door wouldn't go away. The doorbell rang again. Then, there was loud banging on the front door, so Howard finally pulled his pants up and went to the door. He stood near the door, and in his meanest, drunken voice yelled, "Who is it?" It was Mr. W., Howard's friend.

He said, "I need to talk to you and Hazel."

Howard growled, "Come back later. Hazel is not here."

He tried to get rid of him, but Mr. W kept on banging. Howard opened the door just a little and began talking, and Mr. W asked him what was wrong. His friend tried to come inside, but their conversation faded away as I crept into the kitchen. Without a coat, hat, or gloves, I ran. With one sock on and no shoes, I bolted out of the back door into the back yard and over the fence. I ran through our neighbor's backyard onto Silverpine Drive. I ran past all the kids playing in the snow. I ran as fast as I could. I ran for my life to my grandma's house, to safety. That was how it ended. There was no more molestation, no more pretending after that day, but the fear remained for years, well into adulthood. The fear remained even after Howard died. I lived with the kind of fear children should never know, in fact, even an adult should never know that kind of fear. Every time *the molestation* happened, I wanted to run, but I was always paralyzed with fear. The day I finally ran, I think I was hysterical. I guess I had reached some type of emotional breaking point, and my young mind couldn't take the abuse anymore. I believe God knew I'd reached a breaking point and ended it for me that day.

That same day, a man we called Uncle, a family friend, was visiting my grandmother. When I walked inside, I remember the adults asking me, "Jackie what happened to your mouth? Who did this to you? Where is your coat? Where are your boots? Who did this to you?" With fear still gripping me at first, I could not speak. I was so afraid and cold. I whispered with blood flowing down my tee shirt, "Howard."

Then, I collapsed. The next thing I remembered was my grandmother holding me in her arms on her couch. She was crying, and Uncle was telling my mother in his deep policeman's voice, "Hazel if you don't report this, I will. I have to. Uncle had often encouraged Mama to leave Howard, but she never listened to him or anyone else, not when it came to advice about Howard. Many of our family members believed Howard used witchcraft to control Mama. I also remember the man Grandmother lived with, Jose Rios, getting his gun and pretending to protect me that day. The irony of that act is that he was molesting me too regularly. On the basement stairs, he'd pull down my pants and place his adult penis between my little thighs and masturbate. He probably got the gun to intimidate me, so I wouldn't tell what he had done. Jose never touched me again after that day. Uncle was a police officer, and Mama knew he would report Howard and her too if she didn't file a report at the local precinct in Babylon, and so she did. However, she knew it. She'd caught Howard two years earlier and knew *it* had happened before. The next day Mama took me to the precinct. I tried to act like I was brave and smart. When the detective asked me if Howard had intercourse with me, I said, "Yes."

My Mother said, "I don't think she even knows what intercourse is." You could tell by the look on her face she instantly hated me. She didn't know Howard told me the meaning in a drunken stupor while trying to molest me. The police officer at the precinct told Mama to take me to a doctor. I remember her sort of hyperventilating, but she took me to a doctor. She was so relieved when the doctor told her I was still a virgin she nearly fainted. She had to sit down for a few minutes, and the doctor gave her a glass of water. Although he was given many, many opportunities, I thank God Howard never entered my little body.

One night in the woods near 43rd Street, he slurred, "We're going to have intercourse tonight, and sooner or later you are going to have a little baby." I was a little girl in elementary school very frightened and confused when I asked him, "What's enter cause?" I was trying to distract him. He answered boldly, "It's sex, f____king. It's sex between a man and a woman, and you are going to do it."

Now, I really didn't understand. It was the 60's, and like a lot of kids, I was completely naïve about sex. I didn't understand sexual relations between a man and a woman. And I most assuredly did not understand the disgusting sexual urges of a child predator. I didn't know their sick urges escalate, but I did know there was something terribly wrong this time. So, I just shut down, stopped talking to him, and sat frozen on the floor of the back seat hugging my knees tightly to my chest. I sat terrified, thinking about how close 43rd Street was to Great Neck Road. I bowed my head and waited for him to hit me. Like many times before, God caused him to fall into a deep sleep until daylight. That morning when he woke up, like always, he promised me he'd kill Mama if I told anyone. Then, he drove home as if nothing happened. He would often wake up and drive me home at 4:00, 5:00 or 6:00 a.m., and Mama never said a word.

Another night, at about 1:00 am, a police officer stopped and shined a flashlight into the dark car as we sat near the old Convent. When he asked me if I was being held against my will, I remembered Howard's threat that he'd kill my Mama, and I quietly said no. Most mothers would have been suspicious night after night but not mine. My mother didn't protect me. In fact, she placed me in harm's way over and over again. Her number one concern was whether or not Howard had been with any other women. That was the only question she asked. My father was alive then, but he didn't protect me either. He just left. I had no protection except the Lord, Jehovah-

Nissi (*The Lord God Our Banner*). I praise God He is really all the protection I needed. Consider how deeply sick and depraved it is to violate an innocent child, and isn't it just as sick to know that your innocent child is being violated and not protect them. My mom wasn't the worse parent, but let's face it, she had her own deep-seated issues. She was smart but had zero self-esteem and absolutely no clue how to be a responsible parent.

When I was 3 or 4 years old, I thought Howard was my new Daddy. I loved and trusted him at first. I called him, "Howie," and I thought he was wonderful, but he was wicked. Parents always guard and protect your children. They are God's gift to you. Parents never get drunk or party so hard that you don't know where your kids are. Sadly, that was my mom's legacy. She loved to party, and for many years, she was a functioning alcoholic who rarely, if ever, gave any thought to her children or our safety. She didn't know how to show love and protect us because she lived a crazy life, and maybe she didn't even know it was crazy. She certainly never made any real effort to get out. Mama hit the number while I was in the 9th grade. She won $10,000 dollars. In 1969, that was more than enough money for a fresh start, but it never occurred to her. When asked if she would leave, she refused to answer. Clearly, she did not love herself. One of the most powerful (if not the most powerful) life lesson I've learned is to love and honor Jackie. You can start with something as simple as giving yourself grocery store flowers on pay days. You can save for that special piece of jewelry or a quiet weekend get-a-way. Small steps bring big results when the small steps are positive and consistent. Be encouraged. You can be free, and you can have a great life.

I remember my therapist saying she'd love to get into my mother's head and hear her thoughts. I thought, *me too*. For many years, I've wondered how a mother could continue a relationship with the man who she knew molested both her children. It is 2022, and I'm sorry, but I still cannot answer that question.

Because the charges had been filed at the local precinct, Howard was arrested. So, we moved to my aunt's house and later to a basement apartment Howard found us. That brief reprieve didn't last long; in no time at all or at least that's how it seemed to me, we were right back on Great Neck Road. Howard never touched me again, but I didn't know the molestation was over, so I still lived in fear every day and every night. When we moved back to Great Neck Road, Mama no longer slept in their bedroom. She slept on the couch for years. I don't know if she was watching out for me, or if she was so repulsed by Howard that she couldn't lie next to him. She stopped kissing and hugging him too. She was an excellent cook and loved cooking everything from scratch. Mama still cooked every day, but I noticed there didn't seem to be any joy in it for her anymore.

Because I was still a virgin, everyone in my family, except my sister, thought I was lying. Everyone knew I went from loving Howie (the only father I'd known) to hating him with an abnormal intensity. Instead of wondering why such a drastic change in me, why I suddenly hated him so intently, I became the child who lied about s-e-x. Because I was still a virgin and about to start 7th grade, my mother did not press charges.

I saw Uncle one more time. I was in high school by then, and we only talked briefly. I guess he couldn't risk his career getting involved any more deeply in my mother's mess or spend any time with the child who lied about s-e-x. As for me, I was still scared all the time because I didn't know when Howard was going to molest me again or kill Mama so he could molest me all the time. I had headaches that mimicked migraines and thoughts that made me feel sick to my stomach all the time. One day as I sat in health education class, I began to understand what really had been happening to me. I lived daily waiting for him to grab me by the throat again and was especially frightened when he would get up during the night and walk past my bedroom to go to the bathroom. One night, I was so scared I broke out in a cold sweat. I lay awake for hours, terrified and shivering in my bed. My pillow was wet from my tears, but I didn't leave my bedroom at night. By then, Lucille was safe, married to Ben, but like me she was broken. And like me, she was ticking.... Feed the kids. Tick. Do the laundry. Tick. Go to the supermarket. Tick. Plan dinner. Tick. Have another glass of wine. Tick. Plan to kill Howard. Tick. It went on until sadly she became an out-of-control, angry, suicidal, alcoholic and was diagnosed with manic-depressive disorder. All of that ended when Lucille accepted Jesus.

When I was around 12 years old, my Aunt Kitty took me to a holiness church, and that experience planted the love of Christ in me.

"Train up a child in the way he should go And when he is old, he will not depart from it" Proverbs 22:6 NKJV.

There was lots of singing, shouting, and speaking in tongues. There was an organ, a drummer, tambourines, and someone even played an old washboard. By the time I was thirteen years old, I'd taught myself the Lord's Prayer and visited the churches my friends attended. I prayed the Lord's Prayer every night. When I was 14, I started crossing days off on calendars in my bedroom. I crossed off every single day for four and a half years. During that time, I tried to be as normal as I could. But inside, I still lived in constant fear, and I was an angry, ticking time bomb. Tick. Don't ever be late for school, its safe there. Tick. Try to be normal. Tick. Try to have fun. Tick. Get good grades. Tick. Try to make friends Tick. Go to the hookie parties, Tick. Join the drill team. Tick. Join the drama club. Tick. So glad I'm popular. Tick. Act like you have confidence. Tick. Join the track team. Tick. Plan Howard's death. Tick. Complete college applications. Tick. In the midst of all the private ticking during high school, I continued to go to church with friends and even became a member of a local church. I liked church. It felt right even then. Yes, even as I slept in the devil's lair, ticking- church felt right.

I thank God He spared me the actual rape at the hands of Howard Parks or Jose' Rios. The man most people believed was my grandfather we called him Uncle Joey. Quietly, I hated him just as much as I hated Howard, but if no one believed me about Howard, what sense did it make to tell anything else? Tick. *They both should die tick, tick, tick......*

There were two little girls who didn't get away from Howard. He was dating (for lack of a better word) their Mother. They lived on East Street; in fact, I knew her son. He was a quiet kid, nice and friendly. He was in a special education class. One night, Howard went to their house while the Mother wasn't home and raped both little girls. He was arrested. While he was in jail, their mother brought the little girls to our house.

When Mama answered the door, the woman said, "I want to show you what your husband did."

My mother said, "You should know all about him, you are f----ing him."

The lady said, "You are right, and this is my fault, but please allow me to show you what he did." Mama opened the screen door and let them come in. The little girls were about three and four or maybe five years old. They were dressed so nicely, and they both looked so cute. After Mama let them in, she told me to go in my room, and migraines and thoughts that made me feel sick to my stomach all the time. One day as I sat in health education class, I began to understand what really had been happening to me. I lived daily waiting for him to grab me by the throat again and was especially frightened when he would get up during the night and walk past my bedroom to go to the bathroom. One night, I was so scared I broke out in a cold sweat. I lay awake for hours, terrified and shivering in my bed. My pillow was wet from my tears, but I protected me and Lucille too, when no one else did. I'm 68 years old now. By the time this book is published, I will be 69 years old, and my heart still aches for those two sweet little girls. Howard blamed their brother, and I guess their Mother dropped the charges because she felt their family had been through enough. I remember talking to the boy and telling him, "I knew Howard did it."

He said, "Jackie be careful. Howard is evil."

Then, he thanked me quietly and soon after, their family moved away. Howard often got away with doing a lot of really bad things in Amityville because he was a mason, a police informant, and he was a warlock.

Early one morning, Lucille and I both heard him chanting to the devil. Many people in Amityville thought he was dangerous and avoided him. To my whole family and close friends, he was the epitome of evil. The molestation happened most frequently in the wooded area near the old Convent. Howard even tried to molest me right across the street from a classmate's house. Several times, I almost found the courage to run to her house, but a voice in my head said, "What will your classmate and her family think when they answer the door? What if he catches you before you get to their door? He will kill your mom." So, I sat as still and quiet as I could, barely good grades. Tick. Try to make friends Tick. Go to the hookie parties, Tick. Join the accomplish the evil deed that happened to the two little girls on East Street.

Repeatedly, I'd watch him hit my mother for what seemed like hours with his fists because there was lint on the carpet, or his food wasn't hot enough. I knew first-hand how violent he was. And then there was *the threat*. Howard dug a six-foot hole in our backyard. He told our neighbors it was for a second septic tank, but he told me it was for my mother. If I told anyone what he was doing to me, he said he would kill Mama and bury her in that hole, and when people would ask about her, he would say, "She left us." Therefore, I never told anyone, not even my closest friend, Robin.

Even after I ran to Grandma's house, and some of the horror was exposed, the hole was there for years. Every time I went outside to play or visit friends, I would run as fast as I could past the hole in the backyard. As I watched him beat my mom mercilessly nearly every weekend, I believed he would kill her. He certainly beat her near death many times. I was so scared, and Mama was scared too, all the time. She knew Howard was an extremely dangerous and evil man. He worshipped Satan and would openly curse God. He proudly used witchcraft and encouraged my mother and others to do the same. Those beatings continued the entire time we lived there, and it was why our house never really felt like a home.... Because home in my mind then and now is *a safe and happy place.*

Mama grew up in the church. On some level, Mama knew all she needed was Jesus. Even more so, I thank God Aunt Kitty knew to seek Him. You may be wondering why God didn't get her out. Well, God gave her many opportunities, but God will not force himself on anyone. He allows horrific things to occur based on the choices we make, but He will be with you every step of the way through the horror, and Mama knew that much about God. When a woman or a man is intimate with another human being, she did not know they take into themselves the spirit or spirits that companion person is housing. It is called a soul-tic. And clearly something sick and evil tied my mother to Howard, but she was bound long before she met him. Sadly, that made her a good candidate for abuse. Howard loved and embraced evil.

One night when I was 6 or 7 years old, I was peeking around the corner near the kitchen because Howard and Mama were arguing. I saw him hit her again and again with his fists. As old as I am, I still remember the sound of his fists hitting her, but Mama kept fighting, she always fought. When he let her go, she lay down on the couch. Suddenly, Howard picked her up, lifted her above his head, and slammed her onto the floor with such force that her last scream sounded like a wounded animal. Mama stopped fighting and lay very still. I ran to my closet and hid. Howard planned the attack, most batterers do.

Domestic violence is not an out-of-control instance or outburst, and it is not a reflex reaction. Batterers always make a conscious decision to hurt the person with whom they are involved. He began by lying and telling Mama someone told him my father was in Amityville, and she had been seen talking and laughing with him. He didn't know my father probably hated my mother, as he had vowed never to speak to her again. Howard said people told him she had been switching her "a_ _" around him in the bar, and everybody *on the block* had seen them together. Now Mama had a distinctive sexy walk back then, and Howard ended it that night. I believe he intended to paralyze her. She walked with a pronounced limp until her death in 1996. A batterer's need to control is dangerous, obsessive, and it only becomes worse over time. Howard had been beating her regularly, but he really wanted her dead. Both my aunts told me, even before she met him, Mama had developed a pattern of getting involved with crazy violent men who beat women mercilessly.

After Mama came home from the hospital with a broken hip, my family from Brooklyn came to visit. Mama told everyone she fell off the back steps. They all whispered they knew that was a lie. When it was time for the family to leave, everyone went outside to look at the back steps. Howard said he would have a handrail built for the back steps, and my great aunt Mary must have had enough. She yelled, "You filthy liar. I know you did this to my niece. You are a worthless piece of trash and an ignorant low-class bastard! You are a lying coward and a menace to society." She went on to say he should be locked away for life in an asylum for the criminally insane. "I wish you would hit me one time. It will be the last time you raise your hand. Please hit me you son-of-a-bitch, and you will die tonight."

I remember being so scared and waiting for him to hit her, but he didn't move. He didn't say one word. My Uncle Charlie and my Uncle Sammy moved and stood at Aunt Mary's right and my Uncle Lloyd and Uncle Dick stood at her left. When I got older, I understood why he didn't hit her. She would have killed him that night, and he knew it. He knew she really wanted to kill him. If she didn't kill him, my uncles would. Howard, like most batterers, only preyed on weak women and children, especially little girls. All batterers have a dangerous and unhealthy need to control while pedophiles have preferences, sick depraved sexual preferences. The combination of the two is always, always twice as deadly! He loved to inflict pain on people, especially my mother. He seemed to enjoy beating her. I remember the sound distinctly like it was yesterday, and I'm still nauseated by the memory.

Mothers, please take time to get to know a person before you even introduce them to your children. Fathers, don't leave your children uncovered ever by assuming grandparents and other family members will protect them. As beautiful, smart, and kind as my grandmother was, she was never aware that her man, Jose Rios, was molesting me at the very same time as Howard. Jose' Rios was never violent with me. He was a different type of pedophile. He pretended to love me and lured me with candy, fruit, and gifts. Like many child predators, he acted like what he did was our secret game. Yes, long before the hit movie *The Amityville Horror*, unbelievable horror lived in the form of a demon possessed, Satan worshipping, evil, twisted, sick and depraved, drunken hateful, despicable, pedophile warlock, named Howard Parks and his unwitting and equally depraved counterpart Jose' Rios. Sadly, my mother didn't know how to protect me, Lucille, or herself. She also didn't know how to get us away before it was too late.

Molesting a child is nearly as horrific as child rape, and it is still sexual assault. Even without the horror of forced entry, the child is irreparably damaged. The memory remains into adulthood, through college, marriages, and careers.

The National Center for Missing and Exploited Children receive 29 million reports of suspected child sexual exploitation every year.

When all of the madness in our lives was taking place, I always thought our neighbors knew what was happening and were either too scared to help or just didn't care. When I was in my late thirties me, Lucille, and our next-door neighbor, R, were hanging out, and we started talking about why Lucille got married so young and how much we hated all the partying at our house. We told her, "During all the adult partying and drunken brawling, Howard tried to violate us both repeatedly, and our

Mama knew but did nothing." I still remember the shock and sadness on her face because she did not know. She was so hurt for us that she began to cry. She was beyond angry with my mother, and she confronted Mama that same day. She'd always respected Mama as many people in Amityville did. Her mother, Ms. M, and Mama were best friends. Ironically, when Howard got old and was wasting away in severe and constant pain from cancer, it was Ms. M who spoon fed him when he was too weak to lift a spoon. Why she helped him? I do not know, but I do know Ms. M became a born-again believer. I recall her saying, "Jackie, I'm so proud of you, finishing school, working for the mayor and active in your church. Sweetheart, if it's any consolation to you, Howard suffered. I mean he really suffered until he finally died."

Chapter 2

The Middle Passage

When we were little kids, my grandmother went to Maryland to visit friends. While she was there, she saw Howard's picture on a WANTED poster in the post office. He was wanted for MURDER and of course she told my mother, but Mama still stayed with him. Both of my aunts asked, "Hazel are you going to wait until he kills you too?" It may seem unbelievable but my mother ignored my grandmother and both her sisters concerns and she stayed with Howard until I was 35 years old. He beat her mercilessy for 30 years. After that, he replaced her with a younger woman who he later beat to death in that same house on Great Neck Road. In fact, he was indicted for murder, but he died before the case went to trial. He moved the woman and his child into the house on Great Neck Road. After months of my sister and I pleading and prodding, Mama finally left. I believe my mother escaped the death Howard planned for her because she grew up in the church. Even though she rarely acted like it, she knew the Lord. Most of all, thank God, the Lord knew her and protected her. Have you ever heard the saints say, "He will keep you when you don't want to be kept?" That saying is the truth.

Sometimes after Howard would beat my mom, she'd have difficulty standing or walking. Her body would be black and blue with cuts and bruises, or her eye would be swollen shut. I would try to talk her into leaving. Oftentimes, I'd have to help her up off the floor onto a chair or into bed. She'd spit out blood and one or two of her teeth. I can't honestly categorize my mom as a person who didn't know the Lord. She said she grew up in the church, but I often wonder what she was actually taught about trust and faith in God. When I'd question her about why she put up with how Howard treated her, she'd always say, "Don't you worry about that little one. My God is a just God, and He pays every man according to his deeds." Mama's actions were wrong, but her thoughts about the power of God were correct. God is omnipotent and omniscient. He has all power; He is all knowing and all seeing. There is no force, being, or entity greater or more powerful than God and nothing takes Him by surprise. God is just. He also expects us to use wisdom.

By now, you may be wondering, *Why did you choose to tell this horrific and surreal story?* I have a good life now, and surely the Lord has blessed me mightily. In fact, I've forgiven Mama, my Father, Howard, and Jose.' Truthfully, I was glad, and in fact, relieved when Howard and Jose' died. To date, I feel no sadness about either of them. They are no longer renting space in my head or my heart, except that no one prevented the horrific rape of two innocent tiny little girls. Lucille and I even went to Howard's pitiful funeral. At that time, I needed to see him lying in a casket, maybe Lucille did too. Even though we were both saved, it was almost as if we had to be sure that the Lord had taken him off the planet. I remember one my friend's saying, "Jackie, God let you see the end of your enemy."

At the funeral, the minister who preached Howard's eulogy really struggled to find something good to say. She could only say he was a hard-working man. Lucille noticed there were only about 15 people in the entire church, including the clergy, the guests, the choir, and us. Someone bought some grocery store flowers and laid them on top of the casket. We called Howard's son. He was like a real brother to us. We let him know his father died, but he said he didn't want to come. Howard had treated him and his Mother horribly too. When it was time to view the body, I stood at the casket, immobilized, and had to fight the urge to spit on him. I had never spat on anyone in my life. I stood there so long glaring at his dead body that the people in the church thought I was grief stricken. Lucille knew and gently guided me back to my seat.

Only one of Howard's cousins came, and she explained that she only came because of her late father who was Howard's uncle and a pastor. Her dad was a kind man and had often encouraged Mama and Howard to come to his church, but they never went. Lucille and I went to visit her after the services, and we talked about the pitiful funeral. I remember Howard's cousin saying his funeral was a testimony of how he lived. Lucille and I agreed and remarked that it was so obvious that the preacher struggled to find something good to say, and the choir clearly did not want to sing for such a wicked man. I sat in her beautifully decorated home thinking, as I often had, that Howard had such a nice family. What happened to him that made him embrace such evil? We had a nice visit and talked about how grateful we were to be born-again believers. She knew that Howard had beat my mother "breakfast, lunch, and dinner," and his family members always tried to get him to stop, to reason with him, but he never listened. Just before we left Howard's cousin asked with concern, "What ever happened to the little girl, Hazel and Howard had? I smiled and answered, "I'm the little girl." She looked so relieved and said, "Yes, Jackie! Oh, thank God, you made it!" We hugged and promised to keep in touch, but because the memories of all Howard had done to us were too painful back then, we didn't keep in touch. She was so kind.

I pray she is well. I often refer to myself as *"Radically Blessed"* because I am. And a long time ago the Lord spoke to my heart and said, "Tell the people what I've done for you." I'm sharing this part of my life because what God has done for me, He will do for you too. *"For there is no respect of persons with God"* (Roman's 2:11 KJV).

Another reason is to encourage kids in dangerous situations to get away and tell someone who can help with what is happening. I also drafted this book to warn parents (young and old, male and female) that there are unseen dangers, standing at the ready to literally destroy your children if you don't protect them. No matter how lonely you are or what you think you will gain financially, emotionally, or physically; the end-result is not worth it if you are in relationship with a batterer, a person who has embraced the occult or a pedophile.

I experienced recurring nightmares for nearly fifteen years after the molestation stopped. In 2005 on a lovely evening while walking in Hampton, Virginia, I simply looked up at a tree, and I had a "flashback" so intense that immediately I was transported back to one of those horrific nights near the old Convent in Amityville. I was so impacted by the memory that I couldn't breathe. I tried to force the memory away for a few minutes by practicing therapy techniques. I walked quickly and asked myself this series of questions aloud, "What is today's date, what is your home address? What is your age and what is your social security number? I answered aloud and noticed people staring at me as I walked by, but this time the techniques didn't work. Fortunately, I was near home and able to make it into my apartment. I was so scared. I sat on the floor and hugged my knees tightly to my chest. It felt like the evil had reached up from Howard's grave. I felt like a child again, trapped and scared. Nothing like this had happened to me in so many years. Praise God, the Holy Spirit gave me the presence of mind to call my friend Shante.' When she answered the phone, I could barely explain what was happening to me. It all felt so real, but I wasn't 10 years old. I was 51 years old. After Shante' prayed for me and rebuked that evil off me, I thought why is this still happening? Then, I remembered something I'd been taught in church; Satan will come with full lies and half-truths. He will only use what has worked before. What happened to me was beyond terrible, but it is the truth. It did happen. The full lie was that I was still bound by that evil. I was and I still am a born-again believer. The Bible says I have been made new.

"Therefore, if any man be in Christ, he is a new creature: old things are passed away; behold, all things are become new" (2 Corinthians 5:17 KJV).

I have spent much of my life in pain, and I've worked long and hard to overcome the pain of childhood domestic violence and sexual assault. Praise God, with the help of the Lord, I have overcome it all. What happened used to literally terrify me but not anymore. That was then but this is now, and I am more than a conqueror.

"Nay, in all these things you are more than conquerors through Him that loved us" (Romans 8:37 KJV).

When parents remain in abusive relationships or continue involvement with people practicing any form of the occult or when parents remain involved, even after they suspect an adult is being sexually inappropriate with their children, the parent gives that child a lifelong sentence of danger and despair. They risk death for themselves and their children. If you even suspect it, leave. If the violence happens once, it will happen again. End the relationship quick, fast, and in a hurry. Get away, don't delay! Even if you have to leave your own home, you can return at another time. Be Safe First Please!

It took me a very long time to start writing this book and nearly as long to finish it. God was very patient with me. God really is awesome! I wanted to immediately obey God and start writing, but the very thought of re-living my childhood and young adult life were so incredibly overwhelming that, at first, I could not begin. Praise God, He knows my heart, and He gave me time. He gave me grace. I am not defeated nor am I a victim. I am a victor in Christ Jesus. *"And they overcame him by the blood of the lamb and the word of their testimony" (Revelations 12:11 KJV).*

As a teenager, I did a lot of necking and heavy petting, but I intended to save my virginity until marriage. However, during my first semester in college, I got pregnant at age 19 by a pimp's son. After a late term abortion, my days were filled with sadness, confusion, emotional imbalance, drug experiments, and on-going promiscuity. Day after day, I was fueled by fear, shame, guilt, rage, and self-hatred. I had thoughts of suicide and dreams of killing Howard. Ticking like a time-bomb, my hatred for him was so intense that it consumed me and nearly killed me instead. I tried to ease my pain the only way I knew. I became carefree, which to me meant never showing the pain. You see I was searching for something or someone to ease the pain of being unprotected, beaten, and repeatedly sexually assaulted as a child. Most psychologists would say I suffered from post-traumatic stress disorder because of the repeated domestic violence and molestation. When an adult has any sexual contact with a child, it is a sexual assault. I was trying to stop the pain by any means. I even tried alcohol but didn't like hangovers. I tried men and drugs and became addicted to both.

For many years, I suffered with insomnia. When I did sleep, my dreams were filled with terrible memories and repeated scenes of Howard killing me or me killing him. There was so much demonic activity in my dreams and when I was awake until most days I wasn't really here. As most girls do, I internalized the pain. As a young woman,

I stepped effortlessly into the generational curse my Mother and Father's choices pronounced over my life. Howard repeatedly told me, "You will never be nothing. You ain't going to be nothing but a stupid whore just like your mother." My father spoke no words. He was simply absent, just gone, yet his absence spoke volumes. Subconsciously, I believed the self-fulfilling prophecy that I heard almost daily, and it went into effect early in my life.

Chapter 3

Spiraling

By the time I was 20, I was accepted into a 4-year baccalaureate program at Long Island University (LIU), so I moved to Brooklyn or to "the city" as Long Islanders say. At age 21, I was introduced to cocaine. I graduated from LIU. At 23, I met a young man; we became friends and fell in love. We lived together for 17 years. Things got better for me, but it was as in the Tale of Two Cities: "It was the best of times, and it was the worst of times."

We decided to live together. It was unusual and quite unacceptable to live together and not be legally married in 1980. He came from a nice southern family and had some minor issues as all young people do but generally was a likeable guy. Because of my low self-esteem, I continued to experiment with cocaine, and I spiraled downward year after year. He tried valiantly to save me, but only can Jesus save. All illegal/illicit drugs carry very dangerous spirits. I had no idea the new danger I'd put myself in. We started out as neighbors, just chatting about work and the weather in the elevator and later became friends. During this time, I had a "sugar daddy" about 30 years my senior because my mother told me, "Instead of giving it away free, you'd do better to get paid. "It's better to be an old man's darling than a young man's fool" were her exact words.

I stepped effortlessly into the generational curse my Mother and Father's choices pronounced over my life. Howard repeatedly told me, "You will never be nothing. You ain't going to be nothing but a stupid whore just like your mother." My father spoke and the drug induced reality of each day. I hid my habit and functioned for years, but I didn't know the devil was making sure the generational curse that was clearly on my mother stuck to my sister and me. So, I was a well-spoken, educated, and well-paid addict. Just like I thrived in academia, I thrived in business. I made a lot of money to fund my ever-growing habit. In the beginning, I thought I was having fun. I was young, attractive. On the surface, it seemed as if I was living a good life. And for 16 years of my life, I was addicted to cocaine, and it was not good.

Chapter 4

Deliverance

When I was a kid, *playing numbers* wasn't legal, but many people in the African American community played anyway. Many were hoping to *hit it big* but few did! My mom played numbers every day, several times a day, and in the evenings. She *hit* or won almost every week. In fact, she paid my junior college and undergraduate tuition with money she won playing numbers."When I was in 9th grade, Mama won $10,000 dollars. She made me count the money every day for a week until I finally convinced her to open a savings account.

Again, ten thousand dollars was more than enough money to get away back in 1969, but it never occurred to her. By then, I knew I'd be leaving long before she did. And I did, I left Amityville in 1973, at age 19, and I did not return for years. But my reasons for going to college really had little to do with academics. College was my way out. After the molestation stopped, Howard continued to verbally abuse and debase me for 12 more years. One time, he actually pulled a gun on me. The paradox of my mother living with a mad man (like it was normal) completely overwhelmed me sometimes, even as an adult. In many ways, Mama was such a good person with a kind heart. Most people would tell you that Mama would stop whatever she was doing, no matter what time of the day or night. She would help someone if she could and that was true. She'd cook an eight-course meal for a bum without being asked. My Aunt Kitty used to say, "Hazel will give you the coat right off her back, but she will also give you a pain in the rear end."

In 2006, the U.S. Census Bureau reported an amazing 10.4 million single-mother families in this country, and I can't help but wonder how many little girls and boys are living a great life because their mother's chose safety and how many others are trapped in horrific similitude to my young life. Fathers, be sure to also guard and protect your little ones. Don't just disappear and ignore the God-given responsibility of taking care of your gift, your children, like my father did. God is so faithful that I have forgiven my father, but I will never condone his actions or lack thereof.

As of the publication of this book, one in three girls and one in six boys in the U.S. are molested before age 18. Most are molested by someone they know and trust. Parents, I know you aren't comfortable with those stats. I'm sure you are not comfortable with the thought of a grown man or woman assaulting your child, so be sure your children are safe, and don't leave them behind. If you are in a dangerous relationship, it may be difficult to know who to trust. You will need a written plan, and you will need a safe place to keep your plan. Never keep your written plan at home, and whenever possible, plan to take your children with you. For years, I continued to spiral deep into addiction and to feel unworthy of love.

One day I prayed and asked God to send my first love someone else, someone who would love him better than me. And God answered my prayer. God gave him someone else, and he is happily married. I've often heard it said that you should be careful what you pray for. I agree for a host of reasons. Sadly, I remember the exact day and the events that ended our 17-year *relationship* for good. On that day in November 1992, there was a different look on his face as he walked out the door. Somehow, I knew he wouldn't try to save me anymore. After putting food in the refrigerator, he fed the cat, but he left the keys to my apartment on my desk. I continued to shovel cocaine up my nose. I listened to Satan when he told me I could not live without cocaine, and there was no way out. The devil told me to ingest enough cocaine to stop my heart. That's just what I did. I ingested one full quarter of an ounce of cocaine. I should be dead but God.

Instead of the usual hyperactivity and rapid heartbeat I experienced from using cocaine, I lay down and quietly said to God, "If I have to live like this, God, I don't want to live." By then, I knew I was addicted, but I did not know what to do or how to stop using. I didn't even believe I could stop. The Holy Spirit spoke to me that day and asked, "Do you really want to die?" I didn't know it was the Holy Spirit, but I was accustomed to hearing voices and answering them, so I answered, "No." I noticed my heartbeat was slow. I lay down, and when I closed my eyes, I could see a very small light that resembled the flame of a candle which had almost gone out. After a short time, I sat up, opened my eyes, and looked at the coffee table. My first love had left his grandmother's Bible.

As I reached for the Bible, I remembered my Aunt Kitty's words, "If you ever get in trouble, I mean real trouble, read Psalm 23." So, I began there, and by the time I had read part of Psalm 25, I got up, prostrated myself on the floor, and I began to weep. I cried so hard I left puddles on the hard wood floor. I was so tired of using drugs. I had lost my man, several jobs, and most of all, I had lost me and all my hopes and dreams for a good future. While I was prostrate on the floor crying and in despair, God came into the room and touched me. He pulled the spirit of addiction out of the top of my head. Now, to some readers that statement will sound very *Ooky spooky or even crazy*, but if you have ever had a visitation, you will know what I experienced. I was prostrate, yet I could see a long green spirit, and God pulled and pulled until it was out. When I finally sat up, I was different. In fact, I've never been the same. I had been delivered from sixteen years of addiction. Just a few days before, I had a dream that the devil was chasing me. He was trying to kill me, but God whisked me away in a tornado. I shared my dream with one of my neighbors. He was a polite man and a born-again believer. My neighbor told me I was *on a call from God.* I laughed and drank Heineken all day, but God's plan always prevails. I know now that my neighbor was correct, and I have been clean and sober now for 30 years because God always is faithful, and He always has the final say. Just a few days later, I prayed the repentance prayer, and I began to live. I give drugs absolutely no thought, and God keeps me daily. Once a year, I have a beer with my cousins at our family reunion, and that's enough for me. God's plan for my life does not include any addiction.

In 2007, I became a single adoptive parent of my two very beautiful great-nieces. I can't help thinking about how I held this book when they were tiny, precious, little baby girls. I was waiting for them to get older. They have blossomed into remarkable young ladies and have encouraged me to share this story. I can honestly say our life has been really good. We've met some hardship but surely, we are still *radically blessed*.

My life did not change until I accepted Jesus. One evening before the visitation, one of my dear friends from LIU asked her husband to walk me home after a drug binge. While we were walking, he said, "Jackie, those drugs will take you nowhere fast. I know sometimes they seems like fun, and they can even seem harmless, but you know it's very dangerous. I know you don't believe in Jesus, but do me a favor, when you say your prayers just say, 'Father help me please.'" He then said, "Jackie you still trust me, right?"

I answered, "Yes."

Then he said, "Say it for me. Just say, 'Father Help me please." He knew I was *strung-out* and in serious trouble with drugs. He continued, "I know you won't say Jesus so just say Father."

I answered, "Okay, I will."

That night, when I said my prayers, I did as he asked. I know now there was no need to say more. My appointed time had come. I was on my way. My real journey had begun.

God delivered me from drugs in November 1992, just in time for Thanksgiving. I have been clean and sober since that day. I have never been to a drug treatment program or detox facility. I have absolutely no interest in drugs or any desire to use drugs because God ended that for me when I accepted Jesus Christ as my Lord and Savior. I'm grateful my friend's husband didn't judge me, and I'm grateful for how he shared his faith in God with me. We all should do our best to live in a way that doesn't judge others, in a way that does not oppress others because they are struggling or seem different. *"Envy thou not the oppressor and choose none of his ways"* (Proverbs 3:31 KJV).

Chapter 5

The After Glow

For years, in an effort to focus and stay busy, I immersed myself in church, (and I still do). I worked hard. I bought so many gorgeous clothes and way too many shoes. I moved effortlessly into several jobs with great salaries. Did I mention I bought way too many shoes? I stopped smoking cigarettes, and the good taste of food returned. I became a restaurant hopper - not quite a foodie but close. I began to really enjoy the word of God and life. I cannot truthfully tell you I've not had any problems because I've had many. I often say that a Christian's life is peaks and valleys, but again and again, God has been and still is faithful. He always comes to my rescue! Always. He always provides a way of escape! Always. *"But they that wait upon the Lord shall renew their strength; they shall mount up with wings as eagles; they shall run and not be weary; and they shall walk, and not faint" (Isaiah 40:31 KJV).* Know that God's promises are solid, and you can rely on His word. It doesn't matter what manner of evil is done to you. It doesn't even matter if you chose evil. God's plan for your life will prevail. *"No weapon formed against you shall prosper, and every tongue which rises against you in judgment you shall condemn. This is the heritage of the servants of the Lord, And their righteousness is from Me. Says the Lord"(Isaiah 54:17 NKJV).*

I'm not sharing my life story to give Satan any glory. The devil is not worthy of any glory at all. I'm sharing this sad and painful part of my life as a big Hallelujah to Jesus! God has been amazingly good to me. Thank God, I have always been His child. I never, ever belonged to Satan and I never will. I spent years drinking, drugging, and partying like it was *the best thing to do* because there was a deep pain, an empty place in my heart. I first felt it when I was around six years old. A few years after I accepted Jesus, I noticed that pain was gone, and I felt whole.

A decision to use illegal substances or even food to mask, cover, or kill pain is not the best decision. It will lead to a long series of poor choices. We all can have and deserve a balanced life -mind, body, and spirit, but we have to let go of negative patterns and behaviors learned in childhood trauma. I have been blessed to coach many women and girls to let go and achieve their own beautiful versions of balance. I remain humbled by that honor. I'm so grateful for God's plan. No matter where we go, what we do or try, no matter who or what we touch, God has the final say in our lives. He truly is the author and finisher of our faith, and I'm a living witness that God is real. Surely, I would be dead if it were not so. Admittedly, I spent too much of my childhood and young adult life slipping into dark spaces and embracing a negative self-fulfilling prophecy, but that was not God's plan for me, and it is not God's plan for you. Because God is faithful, I made it and you can too. I have learned the hard way. When you use drugs or engage in any activity that is sanctioned by Satan, you make yourself vulnerable. You stop growing and exist in a parallel world ruled by darkness. Today, my heart is filled with gratitude and a true desire to always serve the Lord. I thank God that he gave me salvation and not suicide. I thank God often that I am not HIV positive. I thank God often that I do not have full blown AIDS, and I did not die from a drug overdose.

I lived as an addict for sixteen years. Cocaine was my constant companion, and every evil spirit that accompanied it. I had an intimate and personal relationship with negative forces in the spirit realm, the causal realm. In fact, I've often said I reached over and held the devil's hand. I heard demonic voices daily for years. I engaged in demonic dialogue and did exactly what those evil voices told me to do. I know what madness is because I lived it for way, way too long. The voice that talked the most always whispered, "I love you." That was a lie. The enemy hates humans because God loves us, and we are made in God's image. Thank God His plan for my life and your life is that we will live and live well. Oftentimes it just takes a few small steps to begin the healing process. *"Beloved I wish above all things that thou mayest prosper and be in health, even as thy soul prospereth" (3 John 1:2 KJV)*.

Back in 1992, during my daily walk to the nearest subway, I would feel *a pulling* sensation every time I'd pass a church on Madison Street. By 1993, I had formally accepted the Lord Jesus Christ as my Lord and savior at that church. Under the leadership of the late Archbishop Wilbert S. McKinley, I became an active member of that church, the Elim International Fellowship in Brooklyn, New York. I was baptized there and was filled with the Holy Spirit. This was less than 2 blocks from where I lived on Gates Avenue. As a member of Elim, the generational curse on my life was broken. I met a young deacon who helped birth my first ministry, "the Daughters of Cush." He also helped me with first entrepreneurial efforts.

In 2010, I decided to visit the house I grew up in, the real Amityville Horror house. As I stood in front of the house on Great Neck Road, I noticed the front looked the same, the neighborhood still looked great, and it looked like a nice family lived there. Initially, I felt great fear, then sadness, then nothing. Eventually, I felt joy (because God set me free). I walked away quietly singing with total praise in my heart.

For twenty-two years, I was a proud member of Greater Mount Calvary Holy Church in Washington, D.C. My senior pastors then were Archbishop Alfred Owens and Co-Pastor Susie Owens, and my Associate Pastors were Bishop Cedric Brown and Lady Bobbette Brown. They each sharpened my spiritual acuity and taught me more about what it truly means to be a Christian than words could ever express. I love them, the ministry staff, and the entire congregation of Greater Mount Calvary. I love being a worshipper and follower of Jesus Christ. I love being God's favored daughter and His work-in-progress. I don't bear the burden of my parents' choices anymore, and I don't carry baggage from my past. I am free in Christ Jesus, and I am blessed to be a member of True Worship Deliverance Center now. My pastors are Leon and Veronica Hardy. My pastors lead by example and have taught me to trust the Lord God implicitly and without reservation. I love how the good Lord is all in the details of my life. I love that God rules and reigns. I've been blessed to hold many important positions and enjoy the respect of colleagues and friends, but I am most proud that God allowed me to adopt Desirae and Daryl, my sister's granddaughters. They came to live with me officially in 2007. As of the publication of this book, Desirae is a senior in high school, filling out college applications, and Daryl is navigating life as a junior in high school. I often sit with my morning coffee and wonder where the time went. When did those two little babies grow into these two remarkable, beautiful young women? I love retirement, but I must admit I have enjoyed the interesting coaching opportunities and look forward to hearing from more of you. I try my best to meet each task with integrity and treat the people I serve with dignity, humility, and kindness. Many parts of my life haven't turned out the way I hoped or planned but I can truthfully say I am so grateful that God's plan for my life has prevailed. "*For I know the plans I have for you, declares the LORD, plans to prosper you and not to harm you, plans to give you hope and a future" (Jeremiah 29:11 NIV).*

God has truly been my hope and my help, my safe place, and for sure my resting place. I have survived and even thrived after the horrors of my childhood and very poor decisions of my youth. I have many dear a long-time friends. My closest friend is Rosa. I call her Cookie. She taught me that love and kindness always win. I've loved, I've experienced loss, and I've lived and re-gained it all. I'm still standing on His promises. God faithfully keeps us every day. I try to live my life without regret, and I'm always looking for the next chapter and challenge. *"Therefore, I tell you whatever you ask for in prayer, believe that you have received it, and it will be yours. And when you stand praying, if you hold anything against anyone, forgive them, so that your Father in heaven may forgive you your sins" (Mark 11:24-25 NIV).*

Shortly after I moved to Virginia, the Lord told me, "Your latter days shall be greater than your former days." *"The glory of this latter house shall be greater than the former, saith the Lord of hosts: and in this place will I give peace, saith the Lord of hosts"* Haggai 2:9 *KJV* Surely the word of the Lord is true. I am the quintessential chick from Amityville Long Island that shouldn't have made it, but I did because God has a wonderful plan for my life, and I believe He has a wonderful plan for your life too. I'm still learning to let Him lead. My journey has certainly been long, arduous, excruciatingly painful, and absolutely unfair, but (because I am a child of God) it has also been full of unspeakable joy, happiness, triumph, love, and victory! But like the classic gospel song: "I tell you with certainty I wouldn't take nothing for my journey now."

As I bring this memoir to a close, know that my sister Lucille and I reached a place in Christ where we both knew without any doubt, "We only made it, By His Grace." "*Then Peter replied, I see very clearly that God shows no favoritism*" *(Acts 10:34 NLT)*. Be encouraged beloved and trust God, even when life seems too hard and too unfair to bear. The Bible says you are fearfully and wonderfully made in His image. You can be your best self. You can have a great life. You have power and purpose. Your heavenly Father is King, and you are His favored sons and daughters. "*Thine, O Lord is the greatness and the power, and the glory, and the victory, and the majesty; for all that is in the heavens and in the earth, is thine; thine is the kingdom, O Lord, and thou art exalted as head above all*" *(1 Chronicles 29:11 KJV). To God Be All the glory!*

About The Author

"Beautiful are those whose brokenness gives birth to transformation and wisdom..." – John Mark Green

Jacqueline Williams was born in Brooklyn, New York, grew up in Amityville and attended Long Island University and George Washington University, attaining a B.A. in Psychology and a M.Ed. in Education and Human Development.

Now retired from her career, where she worked as a Special Educator and Advocate for children diagnosed with chronic and terminal illness at one of the nation's top podiatric hospitals, Jacqueline has turned her hand to writing.

Her debut book, By His Grace, is a memoir of her survival of childhood trauma. It is designed to show readers that they are not alone in their fight and can act as a stimulus for conversations that will encourage them to open up about their experiences and help them heal as a result.

Today, Jacqueline lives in South Hill, Virginia, with her sister's granddaughters, Desirae and Daryl, whom she has adopted. She spends her free time power walking, drinking coffee, eating out, reading, and going to the theater and cinema. She also gives back to her community, having designed and run a free youth empowerment program, Who's At Risk? for girls ages 10-20 who have experienced family trauma, bullying and low self-esteem.

In the future Jacqueline is keen to travel, both within the United States and internationally, to talk with other survivors and those who are undergoing the healing process.

You can contact or connect with Jacqueline Williams at:

Facebook: Jacqueline Williams
Instagram: Jackiesbiz
Email: willjac58@gmail.com

Made in the USA
Middletown, DE
16 March 2024